Red Hat® Linux® Fedora™ For Dummies

vi commands

Many people find that working in a text-based environment makes everyday systems administration jobs a little easier. You're likely to work from a CLI terminal emulator (see our comments in Chapter 4 about the GNOME Terminal) after you have been working with Linux for a while. The Visual Editor, vi, is almost as old as the Unix operating system and is much older than Linux. The straightforward text editor vi is nothing fancy, like OpenOffice, but is nonetheless quite useful and powerful.

The following list of commands contains the most useful and commonly used commands to control the vi text editor. We have been using vi for more than 20 years, in fact, and have never had to use many other commands than these — proving that you can be lazy and still get work done.

You can start vi by entering the command vi from the GNOME Terminal shell prompt:

```
[username@somemachine username]$ vi somefile
```

You enter these commands from the vi editor (see Chapter 4 for more details):

vi filename	Open *filename* in vi
I	Enter Insert mode, inserting before the current position
Shift+I	Enter Insert mode, inserting at the beginning of the current line
a	Enter Insert mode, inserting after the current position
Shift+A	Enter Insert mode, inserting at the end of the current line
Esc	Return from Insert mode to Command mode
x	Delete a character while in Command mode
cw	Delete the word to the left of the cursor and put the editor in Input mode
:w	Write out the file
:q	Quit with no additional writes to the disk
:wq	Write back the file, and then quit
Shift+ZZ	Write back the file, and then quit
:q!	Quit the file with impending changes unwritten
/string	Search forward through the file for a string
?string	Search backward through the file for a string
n	Find the next string (either forward or backward)
u	Undo the last command

Red Hat® Linux® Fedora™ For Dummies®

Cheat Sheet

Systems administration commands

The following list shows several commonly used Linux commands that help you to manage disks, shut down your computer, and gather information about your computer system. You enter these commands from a GNOME Terminal shell prompt. Consult Chapter 4 for more information about how to enter commands.

Command	Description
mount [options] device file_system	Mount a file system.
umount [option] file_system	Unmount a file system.
fsck [options] file_system	Check the structure and integrity of a specified file system.
mkfs [options] file_system	Put a directory structure on a low-level formatted disk.
shutdown	Shut down the system now rather than wait for a message to be sent. (Ctrl+Del does the same thing).
vmstat [options]	Look at the virtual memory performance.
procinfo	Gather information about processes.

File permissions

The following examples show different file permission combinations. Consult Appendixes C and D for more information about files and file permissions.

Permission	Description
-rwxrwxrwx	Creates read, write, and execute permissions for the user, the group, and the rest of the world (mode 777)
drwxr-xr--	Creates a directory that is completely open to its owner and that can be read and searched by the group and read (but not searched) by the world (mode 754)
crw-r--r--	Creates a character-special file that the owner can read or write to but that the group and the world can only read (mode 644)
brw-------	Creates a block-special file that only the owner can read and write to (mode 600)

For Dummies: Bestselling Book Series for Beginners

Red Hat® Linux® Fedora™

FOR

DUMMIES®

by Jon 'maddog' Hall and Paul G. Sery

WILEY

Wiley Publishing, Inc.

Red Hat® Linux® Fedora™ For Dummies®

Published by
Wiley Publishing, Inc.
111 River Street
Hoboken, NJ 07030-5774
www.wiley.com

Copyright © 2004 by Wiley Publishing, Inc., Indianapolis, Indiana

Published by Wiley Publishing, Inc., Indianapolis, Indiana

Published simultaneously in Canada

For general information on our other products and services or to obtain technical support, please contact our Customer Care Department within the U.S. at 800-762-2974, outside the U.S. at 317-572-3993, or fax 317-572-4002.

Wiley also publishes its books in a variety of electronic formats. Some content that appears in print may not be available in electronic books.

Library of Congress Control Number: 2003112921

ISBN: 0-7645-4232-X

Manufactured in the United States of America

10 9 8 7 6 5 4 3 2 1

1B/RZ/RR/QT/IN

WILEY   is a trademark of Wiley Publishing, Inc.

About the Authors

Jon 'maddog' Hall is the executive director of Linux International, a vendor organization dedicated to promoting the use of the Linux operating system. He has been in the computer industry for more than a quarter of a century (somehow, that sounds more impressive than just "25 years"), the past 18 years of which have been spent using, programming, and admiring the Unix operating system. Jon works for Compaq Computer Corporation, where he is helping to shape Compaq's strategy with respect to Linux. Previously, Jon was the department head of computer science at Hartford State Technical College, where his students lovingly (he hopes) gave him the nickname 'maddog' as he tried to teach them operating system design, compiler theory, and how to live an honorable life.

While working for Digital Equipment Corporation in May of 1994, 'maddog' met Linus Torvalds, and was intelligent enough (his critics say 'maddog' was just lucky) to recognize the potential of the Linux operating system. Linux changed his life, mostly by providing him with 22-hour workdays. Since 'maddog' has started working with Linux, however, he has also started meeting more girls (in particular, his two godchildren). You can usually find Jon speaking at various Linux conferences and events ('maddog' just barks), and he has also been known to travel long distances to speak to local Linux user groups.

Paul G. Sery is a computer systems engineer employed by Sandia National Laboratories in Albuquerque, New Mexico. He is a member of the Computer Support Unit, Special Projects, which specializes in managing and troubleshooting UNIX and Linux systems.

When he is not beating his head against systems administration problems, Paul and his wife, Lidia, enjoy riding their tandem bicycle through the Rio Grande valley. They also enjoy traveling throughout Mexico. Paul is the author of *Linux Network Toolkit* and the co-author of several other books. He has a bachelor's degree in electrical engineering from the University of New Mexico.

Dedication

Jon 'maddog' Hall: To Mom & Pop (TM), whose aversion to things electronic is well known, and who can still call their son Jon rather than maddog.

Paul G. Sery: To my wife, Lidia Maura Vazquez de Sery.

Author's Acknowledgments

I want to thank my wife, Lidia, for her patience, support, and good advice, all of which have made writing this book possible. Without her, I would still be the pocket-protector-wearing, busted-eye-glass-fixed-with-tape-looking, "Star Trek"-watching, wrinkled-shirt-suffering, spaghetti-in-the-pot-over-the-sink eating, Saturday-night-hacking sorry sorta guy. Well, I never was into "Star Trek," and I *am* pecking at this keyboard on Saturday night, but my beautiful wife sure has made me a better man.

I would also like to thank Anne Hamilton and Laura Lewin, who gave me the chance to write in general and this book in particular. Both showed great confidence and patience in me. I am very grateful and wish them success in their ventures.

And, of course, I want to thank the staff at Wiley Publishing, who provided considerable and essential help, too. Terri Varveris and Rebecca Whitney provided constant and essential assistance.

I want to acknowledge a total lack of assistance in writing this book from my dog, the infamous Oso Maloso; eater of many things that should have ended his long career early, including but not limited to ant poison, Advil, many pounds of Tootsie Rolls one Halloween, several bags of chicken bones at one party, beer, and other assorted items; escaper of many fences and gates; and friend of the late, great Paunchy (whose name you see throughout this book) and other local dogs.

How useful was Oso? Well, one night while working on this book I got a phone call. Leaving my apple pie behind next to the keyboard, I went downstairs to take the call and passed him on his way up. I should have known something was up because he had a cell phone with him and no one answered when I picked up to take the call. I went up the stairs while he went down. The apple pie was gone. Oso 1, human 0.

— *Paul G. Sery*

Publisher's Acknowledgments

We're proud of this book; please send us your comments through our online registration form located at www.dummies.com/register/.

Some of the people who helped bring this book to market include the following:

Acquisitions, Editorial, and Media Development

Project Editor: Rebecca Whitney

Acquisitions Editor: Terri Varveris

Technical Editors: Korry and Susan Douglas

Editorial Manager: Carol Sheehan

Permissions Editor: Laura Moss

Media Development Specialist: Angela Denny

Media Development Manager: Laura VanWinkle

Media Development Supervisor: Richard Graves

Editorial Assistant: Amanda M. Foxworth

Cartoons: Rich Tennant (www.the5thwave.com)

Production

Project Coordinator: Erin Smith

Layout and Graphics: Carrie Foster, Joyce Haughey, Kristin McMullan, Mary Gillot Virgin, Shae Lynn Wilson

Proofreaders: Laura Albert, Carl William Pierce, Charles Spencer, Ethel M. Winslow

Indexer: TECHBOOKS Production Services

Publishing and Editorial for Technology Dummies

Richard Swadley, Vice President and Executive Group Publisher

Andy Cummings, Vice President and Publisher

Mary C. Corder, Editorial Director

Publishing for Consumer Dummies

Diane Graves Steele, Vice President and Publisher

Joyce Pepple, Acquisitions Director

Composition Services

Gerry Fahey, Vice President of Production Services

Debbie Stailey, Director of Composition Services

Contents at a Glance

Table of Contents

Introduction

. . . .

*R*ed Hat Linux Fedora For Dummies is designed to help you install and use Red Hat Linux. This book shows you how to do fun and interesting — to say nothing of useful — tasks with Red Hat Linux. This book is also designed to be an effective doorstop or coffee cup coaster. Whatever you use it for, we hope that you have fun.

About This Book

This book is designed to be a helping-hands tutorial. It provides a place to turn for help and solace in those moments when, after two hours of trying to get your network connection working, your dog bumps into the cable and it magically starts working.

Note: At press time, Red Hat renamed its Linux product to the Fedora Project. Throughout this book, we usually refer to the product as Red Hat Linux. You'll probably see the product referred to as the Fedora Project in the news, on the Web, and elsewhere, but you can rest assured that the different terms, as used in this book, are referring to the same product.

We tried our hardest to fill up this book with the things you need to know about, such as how to

- Install Red Hat Linux
- Get connected to the Internet by using broadband DSL and cable modems or old-fashioned dial-up modems
- Get connected to your Local Area Network (LAN)
- Build a simple but effective firewall
- Build Internet and LAN services, such as Web pages and print servers
- Use Red Hat Linux to play CDs and listen to Internet radio stations
- Use the GNOME desktop environment
- Take advantage of useful and usable applications, such as the OpenOffice desktop productivity suite, Evolution desktop organizer and e-mail client, and streaming multimedia MPlayer.

- ✔ Work with the OpenOffice desktop productivity suite to satisfy your word processing, spreadsheet, and presentation needs
- ✔ Upgrade your computer and network security
- ✔ Know where to go for help
- ✔ Manage your Red Hat Linux workstation

You see troubleshooting tips throughout this book, and Chapter 18 is devoted to the subject. It's not that Red Hat Linux is all that much trouble, but we want you to be prepared in case you run into bad luck.

The instructions in this book are designed to work with the version of Red Hat Linux you find on the companion DVD; we also describe how to download several software packages not found on the DVD-ROMs. Feel free to use other versions of Red Hat Linux or even other Linux distributions, but be aware that our instructions may not work exactly or even at all. Good luck!

Foolish Assumptions

You know what they say about people who make assumptions, but this book would never have been written if we didn't make a few. This book *is* for you if you

- ✔ **Want to build a Red Hat Linux workstation:** You want to use the Linux operating system to build your personal workstation. Surprise! The DVD-ROM in the back of this book contains the Red Hat Linux distribution.
- ✔ **Have a computer:** It's just a technicality, but you need a computer because this book describes how to install Red Hat Linux on a computer.
- ✔ **Have no duct tape:** You want to put the Red Hat Linux operating system and the computer together, and using duct tape hasn't worked.
- ✔ **Don't want to be a guru:** You don't want to become a Red Hat Linux guru — at least not yet.

However, this book is *not* for you if you're looking for

- ✔ **An all-encompassing reference-style book:** We simply don't have enough space, or permission from the publisher, to provide a comprehensive range of topics. We concentrate on providing help with getting popular and useful stuff up and running. We devote more space, for example, to getting your DSL or cable modem working than to describing the the that makes them work.